Living in wisdom -
an examination of human nature

Richard A. Byron-Cox

Copyright © Richard A. Byron-Cox 2025

All Rights Reserved

No part of this publication may be reproduced, distributed, or transmitted in any form or by any means, including photocopying, recording, or other electronic or mechanical methods, without the author's prior written permission, except in the case of brief quotations embodied in critical reviews and certain other non-commercial uses permitted by copyright law. For permission requests, please get in touch with the author.

Contents

ABSTRACT	ii
Dedication	iii
The Intimate Wisdom of the Reviewers	iv
Foreword	xiii
Prologue	xvi
On Character	1
On Courage	16
On Love	27
On Reason	37
On Justice	59
About Religious Faith	66
On Truth	81
On Politics	91
On Friendship	98
On Hate	112
On Living Each Day	122
Afterword	158
Acknowledgement	163

This is Your Book

In this book there is on each page a section titled, "My reasoning is:" There, you the readers are encouraged to write your own thoughts. Your own philosophy for living.

In reading this book and writing your thoughts, you will find yourself wrestling with the views of the author; with your ideas of living; with your own thinking. Because, you are about to discover and interrogate your mind and your living like never before!

ABSTRACT

Battle the currents of the turbulent seas
Walk the challenging hills without murmur
Drink from the streams so that your tears are refilled
Hide in the valley of calm
And always keep climbing to the mountain tops
For living was never meant to be a station, even a comfortable one.
No. Living is in fact a continuous journey through seasons and places that make time meaningful.

Dedication

To Oscar Oramas Oliva

For being

My teacher, advisor, friend, and adopted father

And in memory of

Conrad Sayers

The inspiration that fired my imagination, and my greatest

influence

And

Philbert "Phil" Browne

The greatest friend I have known and will ever know

The Intimate Wisdom of the Reviewers

I really enjoyed spending time with and thinking with the manuscript. I love the participatory nature of the book - making wisdom a shared process, not an instruction. Inviting readers to pause, think, and write — to actively engage with each aphorism — turns the experience from reading into conversation. It's a generous structure that makes the book deeply personal.

I also value how the aphorisms can be approached on their own, or allow several to wash over you and then step back to think. Each one sits comfortably on its own, yet together they form a sustained meditation on human dignity — which, I think, emerges as the book's central moral thread. It brought to my mind Kant's Kingdom of Ends.

It's a rich and inspiring work — full of wisdom to sit with, return to, and argue with. Thank you again for trusting me with it.

James Schneider

Communications Director

The Progressive International

London, England

"Living in Wisdom" is clear and deeply thought-provoking. Dr. Richard A. Byron-Cox shares ideas that many of us hold but are often afraid to express; he challenges us to face reality. As a well-travelled Caribbean man, he brings the best of his experiences back home to uplift our communities and the wider world. This work is a reminder that true change begins within, and if we take the opportunities to be challenged, we can rise to new levels of personal awareness and growth.

Mrs. Villette S. M. Browne

MBA, B.Sc., Accredited Director

Managing Director

VHB Inc | K.P. Holdings Ltd

St. Vincent & the Grenadines

Thank you for the privilege of reviewing this inspiring manuscript. It is a beautifully crafted piece of work—accessible, engaging, and rich in wisdom. Its readability ensures that it can serve as a practical reference point for the everyday person seeking guidance and perspective in navigating the complexities of life.

The structure of the book, with its concise nuggets of wisdom and space for personal reflections, provides a powerful tool for today's busy reader. In an increasingly fast-paced and impersonal world, this design invites moments of pause, self-reflection, and adaptation, which are invaluable for personal growth and resilience.

The book's simplicity is one of its strengths. It makes profound insights approachable even for readers who may not usually engage deeply with philosophical or reflective texts. By blending real-life situations with universal lessons, the manuscript achieves an appealing balance between entertainment and depth, enabling a wide range of readers to find meaning and relevance.

In conclusion, this manuscript is a delightful blend of accessibility and wisdom, offering readers an evergreen resource for life's journey. It has the potential to stand out as both a deeply personal and universally relevant work.

Dr. R. Mawuli Coffie

CEO, Sustainable Solutions Africa

Accra

Ghana

I found it a mixture of emotions to read. I tried to be honest with my comments, although the next time I read, I thought of it in a different way. I suppose because depending upon the mood the mind is in at that particular moment, an alternative view might be seen. It certainly taxed my mind as to what I really thought.

Thank you for your mind blowing read!

Mrs. Jackie West

Kent, England

UK

This is a book which calls for deep introspection and forces one to examine themselves, to gauge how to manage their emotions, and also their interactions with others. This is a book that should be read slowly over a period of time pausing at each quotation and evaluating the questions that each one generates. However, the temptation to keep on turning the pages for the next quotation could not be resisted. Hopefully, after reading this book, the readers will emerge as better human beings.

Mr. Ellsworth I. A. John

St. Vincent and the Grenadines'

Ambassador to Cuba

Havana

Cuba

Dear Richard,

I just finished reading your book.

Most sentences (we would use the term « maxime » in French), merit deep and long thinking to build a personal opinion. This is probably what makes your book unusually special, almost unique, at least rare…

Some sentences are for me common sense, because I share the opinion expressed and could have written the same probably, of course with less writing talent than you, (your mastering of English is in my view exquisite).

In some sections (on Faith particularly), your opinion is very strong and affirmative. Like a challenge to the reader.

For somebody like me who know and love you, a question come again and again to mind: what course of live and experiences brought you to the conclusions you share with your reader, challenging him/her to express his/her reasoning while as writer, you do not explain yours at all?

May be an idea for your next book would be to take the time to write your own story, the intellectual path you had come through and followed to reach your statements on so many compartments of life and human soul… I am sure that it would be a fascinating book.

Sincere gratitude for honouring me by sharing this unique piece of deep thinking

Alain Retiere

Agroecologist &Climate change expert

Douarnenez

France

"Some of the rivers people crossed were made by their own tears." ~ Dr. Richard A. Byron -Cox

The foregoing quote is both thought provoking as well as inspirational. Dr. Byron-Cox's brutal honesty is compelling, captivating and sincere, his words are by no means superficial, they're a candid collection of meaningful life lessons; written by a man of experience, wisdom and integrity. The constant use of the naked truth and the unwavering tone make the messages tantamount to gospel!

"What good is intelligence if one refuses to live intelligently?" ~ Dr. Richard A. Byron-Cox

Though the material is based on the author's life experience, it applies to anyone seeking righteousness, wisdom and purpose.

Mr. Bantu Campbell
Unit Head
Financial Applications and Accounting Unit
Eastern Caribbean Central Bank
St. Kitts

I really like the format that allows the reader to interact with the text. Also, I like that these are original thoughts, not copied and pasted from elsewhere. There are some beautiful turns of phrase.

Bert Providence
Toronto
Canada

First, I wanted to say how honoured I am to be given a preview into this book. As I read the first few quotes I started smiling because I realized how thought-provoking these quotes are, they demand of me to read on and how I tend to relate to them. Although these were your quotes read by me for the first time, it was inspiring to know that many of them were revelations of experiences that I have had in my own journey of life. It was fulfilling because they gave me comfort in knowing that I was on the right track of thought as you have put them together in words easily understandable and identified. My only wish would be that under every quote, you would give a little explanation much like the dictionary would give the meaning of words. But that may not be possible given the intent to have a short read. This book I believe to be one of your most valuable pieces of writing.

Vincent Alexander

Businessman & IT Technician

St. Vincent & the Grenadines

Richard A. Byron Cox- The quintessential Caribbean man, authors his perspectives in a compellingly-authentic, yet deeply philosophically disturbing way- with thoughts that retrace the borders of morality and ethics, descriptive of his spiritual values and underscoring his literary genius.

Lancelot G. J Wills

International Lawyer

Head

Customs petroleum

Georgetown

Guyana

I commend you on the profoundness of the thoughts here expressed. Good luck and thanks for giving me the opportunity to read them.

Mr. Dexter Rose

Journalist & Jazz musician

Kingstown

St. Vincent

I have known Richard A. Byron-Cox since 2010, and ever since, I have found myself inspired by his thoughts that call for deep reflection. Reading this manuscript took me back to those afternoons when he shared his thoughts and when we could discuss philosophical questions; where truth, justice, love, and reason were never abstract ideals but living realities to be wrestled with. His words reminded us that true success is not always found in relentless forward motion, but often in the courage to pause and reflect; that dignity is priceless, and without integrity, intellect itself is empty; that love—especially selflove—is the foundation of our humanity.

These writings reveal how ignorance may be overcome through wisdom, while arrogance, ego, and blind belief remain the real dangers to the soul. They challenge us to reject imposed truths, to confront injustice, and to rise above the noise of slander and folly, always guided by reason and compassion. What Richard A. Byron-Cox offers here is more than a collection of thoughts: it is an invitation to those willing to go deeper into mind, reason, and humanity itself. His teachings will surely endure, not as mere words, but as seeds that awaken courage, humility, and a longing for justice in all who are ready to listen.

Mr. Ahmid Daccarett

Guatemalan Poet

Guatemala City

Guatemala

Thought provoking, daily bread and corner stone of human survival, are some of the words used to describe the book Titled: "Living in Wisdom – An examination of human nature".

On the other hand, the book calls for introspection and self-searching moments which may cause guilt depending on your actions or inactions resulting in injustice or unfair treatment to others.

My outlook has changed after reading the section on hate, in fact, I usually have very strong dislike for people who have done me wrong. Now I have learned to hate the system that keep them there instead of hating them. As such I took the stance to be silent than to be a drumbeater for hate.

The book placed religion under the microscope, the views shared by the author might not be aligned with those of members of the Christian faith/believers. However, until proven otherwise, the facts presented in the book stand.

The book speaks about the truth and the risk of an endangered Revealer who is haunted by the Lier, all of which speaks volume to the practicality and relatability of the book.

In summary, the book is very thought-provoking and inspiring. It has a way of making you pause, think and reflect deeply on your life. I love the fact that it encourages you to use both your heart and your mind, and makes you look at life through various new perspectives.

The author's perspectives on character, love, truth, courage, and justice are very useful for everyday life. What truly makes this book amazing is the fact that it allows readers to engage and write their own thoughts, allowing them to use the book as a journal/diary. This is so great because it allows for the book to be used for both recreational purposes, and as an escape or release. Reading it can make you feel motivated and challenged to change, think and grow. It's quite a useful and enjoyable book, it can be a weapon or a sword, use it to your advantage.

It's a big hit and a mega seller, highly recommended as a collector's item.

Mr. Patrick W. Watson
Snr. Dir. Hazard Mitigation & Risk Management
Ministry of Local Government & Community Development
Kingston
Jamaica

Foreword

Richard A. Byron-Cox is widely known as an international civil servant and a legal luminary. In recent times, he has shifted focus to writing novels. This work offers unadulterated sensibilities expressed through musings. It was Stuart Hall (1932-2014), the Jamaican intellectual who helped found the discipline of Cultural Studies, who noted that Caribbean persons in the diaspora experienced multiple identities. The author's identity is undoubtedly Vincy in this text. By this offering of Vincy philosophy to the global community, he is blazing the trail set by the likes of the religious leader Mother Priam (Victoria Alexandrina Thomas/Priam, 1909-2005), who generations of Vincies have learnt through oral tradition: "It won't be always so!"

Proverbs are indeed a well-established element of Caribbean orality. Ask the Trinidadian calypsonian the Mighty Bomber who sang:

> Me great-great-grandmother, Madam Rubble
> Teach me proverbs and get me in trouble
> She say, "How you make your bed, so you lie."
> And "You never miss the water 'til well run dry."
> The proverb that really trap me, my friend
> is when she told me that, "The longest rope have an end."
> So the next day, I went by me partner, Pope
> I look on the ground, see a piece of rope
> I pull the rope 'til me hand get corn
> Well, I never see rope long so since I born
> But coming to the end when I raise me head
> I had to take off and bawl out, "Oh goord, I dead!"
> The proverb she taught me was so awful.
> At the end of the rope was a big, big bull.

Here is Bomber poking fun at a Caribbean tradition but simultaneously inscribing into the popular memory Caribbean philosophy.

Richard A. Byron-Cox has travelled the route of a primary school teacher through the youth movement to highest level of university training. Although he has moved from the inner city to the global stage, he remains grounded as an organic intellectual.

His wrestling with Western intellectual thought is unsurprising. Not many have reflected on the idea of humanity from the first Caribbean rebel, Hatuey (?-1512), who preferred a place in the afterlife away from Spanish conquistadors. Then, there was Joseph Chatoyer (?-1795), the Garifuna chief and first national hero of St. Vincent and the Grenadines who asked in the late eighteenth century, "What king" to reject British colonialism. We also know that Eric Williams' declined thesis on *Capitalism and Slavery* was dismissed as careless talk. In this text there is neither careless talk nor long talk. It is to the point, yet the philosophical quips are fully loaded.

This text therefore lies solidly within the Caribbean intellectual thought. More specifically, it is in the Vincy tradition of the likes of the Strolling Scribbler. Strolling Scribbler wanted to know if St Vincent had just had just dropped out of the sky, and so insisted there must have been a "discovery" by a fifteenth century Italian navigator Christopher Columbus.

This text also takes the offering by Vincy calypsonian Gerard "Rasum" Shallow (1961-2012) in *Perseverance* to a higher height. Rasum sang, "Never mind the sweet, You got to sweat to get". And he continued: "Every good seed you sow brings a fruit wherever you plant it". All of these are philosophical posturing that John Sterling (1806-1844) had nothing over.

What Richard A. Byron-Cox has done in this work is to plant seeds. The Jamaican poet and novelists Roger Mais (1905-1955) in his "Men of Ideas" assured us:

Men of ideas outlive their times

An idea held by such a man does not end with his death

His life bleeding away goes down into the earth, and they grow like seed

The idea that is not lost with the waste of a single life

Like seed springing up a multitude.

In the prologue, Byron-Cox confesses of his motivation to think big and ask big questions. Long before him, the Vincy writer and editor Orde Coombs (1939 –1984), who had relocated to New York in the late civil rights era, wrote in an article entitled "A Place like home", published in *Black World/Negro Digest* in December 1971:

"And I know now, as I sit at the water's edge and look on the blackness of the river, that one can find order within the chaos of this dazzling city, since the centre that one seeks lies, as always, within oneself."

The 'inward hunger' that drove the author has gifted the world an excellent addition to the body of Caribbean literary works.

Dr. Cleve McD Scott
Historian, cultural critic &
development specialist
Lecture, UWI, Cave Hill
Barbados
23/09/2025

Prologue

Dear Reader,

I decided to write this brief prologue as I think it's necessary for various reasons. Firstly, let me state from the start, this work is not a philosophical treatise in the sense of the European understanding of those terms. Neither is it some abstract, atmospheric, and nebulous theory meant to explain all the mysteries of the multiverse to the wise of this world. Not that those questions are insignificant. Rather, they are not the subject of this book.

My intentions are that this work will serve the purpose of giving you the reader some thoughts on people's behaviours when acting in the various fields covered herein. But of greater significance is that I here will try to explain why I think the subject tackled in this book is important to you personally.

As it says on the very first page, " This is Your Book." I can almost see and hear you wondering: But what does that actually mean? Well, even with that very first line on the very first page, this book is already achieving one of its aims: Getting you to think, to question. This is not to suggest that you don't think or question, but rather to point to that specific objective of this work. Many people exist most of their lives without seriously questioning anything around them. And first and foremost, rarely, if ever, questioning themselves.

Who am I? Why am I here? What is it I am meant to do? Am I doing the best I can do? Am I living according to me, according to my purpose, or according to what is expected of me? These questions and many more are fundamental to the living of a thinking person; to the living of their mind. They are important for the particular reason of assisting in charting one's course for living, and for having an outlook on life and living. Probably, some people don't think about them because they assume they already know the answers. But is this really the case?

The beginning: My struggles in living the life of the mind

From as far back as I can recall, I always had two questions: Who am I? And, why am I here? These have bothered me from the first day I became conscious I had a brain. I further recall the very first time I clearly situated myself in the universe of my thoughts. I was an eight-year old, and had gone to a gospel crusade in the park. Being bored with the sermon, I wandered off and lay on the grass looking up at the sky. It was a dark night and I saw the beauty of what was for me thousands of stars. Suddenly, I felt tinier than a grain of sand, and yet I felt I was the master of this universe, (then, I didn't know that what I was looking at was part of the multiverse). I felt as if I was alone in this huge and magnificent space, and that it all belonged to me, for there was no one else. And suddenly, I thought I had gone crazy, something was wrong with my mind, for I was clearly not alone in the world, and none of this belonged to me. As I write this now, I am remembering this incident and thinking that you the reader may now think that I am probably still somewhat insane. No, I am not! I didn't know it then, but it was the first time I was simply examining myself. It was the moment when I began to live the life of the mind.

I entered university at the beginning of my 20s, and there is when and where I was properly introduced to philosophy as a discipline. Thanks to the late Conrod Sayers, (the greatest influence on my life, and to whose memory, this book is in part dedicated), I had already read a few related works by Francis Bacon, (I now don't recall exactly what), Alvin Toffler (Future Shock and Third Wave), Bertrand Russell (Why I am not a Christian), and Martin Luther King Jr. (Strength to love). Those works set my mind alive to seriously think, and it never slumbered after that. University brought Georg Wilhelm Friedrich Hegel, Karl Marx and many other thinkers to my consciousness, and from then on, I became obsessed with answering one fundamental question: What is the meaning and purpose of my life? Here now is where my determine efforts at self-examination began.

I finished university having not answered that question, but worse still, (depending on one's perspective), coming to the realisation, that I was light years from being educated. At best, my university training was the brainwash required for society to deem me a man of learning. But then these questions came: Was I being me, or just being what is expected of me? And, is there a difference between these two ideas? That was the moment I set out on the journey to get an education in the hope that it will finally lead me to the answers I was seeking.

So have I found the answer? You will determine that after reading this book!

My search and this book

In broad terms, philosophers are said to be either empiricists (Bacon), or rationalists (Descartes). The former are those who believe that the primary source of knowledge comes from observations and sensory experiences. Put simply, they are of the view that our knowledge comes from the objective world (facts), and how our senses perceive those facts. The rationalists on the other hand, postulate that our knowledge comes first and foremost from our ability to reason, and from our innate ideas. This book does not seek to resolve that argument. It is only mentioned here to point out that this work is philosophically speaking, one of empirical-rationalism. I placed observation first, and then tried to understand, or as we say in the Caribbean, put into perspective what I saw, heard, felt, or otherwise became aware of through my various senses. Based on this approach, I began this journey just observing the world around me, nature in all its expressions: trees, rivers, changes in the seasons, the powers of natural disasters, animals, and this list goes on and on.

I soon realised that these expressions of nature, while they form the fundamental material base for my life, my living is essentially me relating to society, that is to say, my interaction with individuals and groups of individuals, (family, friends, neighbours, coworkers, and on and on). And, with institutions, systems, structures, societal morals and rules; be these government institutions, religion, politics, culture, law, and everything else social. It wasn't hard to see that as with individuals, expressions of the collectives, beginning with my immediate neighbourhood, leading all the way to the corridors of power at international organisations and the richest corporations in this world, are the wishes of people. Human beings like me. Consequently, to understand my living, -that is my relating to individuals and society as a whole, I saw that I need to understand people. And so began my careful observations of humans, which is what informs this book.

As I observed, I began to see patterns in behaviours and recurring practices many of which are conditioned by, and also independent of people's religious and political persuasions, upbringing, level of formal training, race and gender. This underlines that there are many, many things that determine people's actions, or indeed non-actions. I began writing down some of these observations, and to ponder upon them. This led me to conclude that I must try to live much more aware, subjecting my living realities to constant interrogation. In this quest I further realised that if I were to consider just the others and not myself, I would be only undertaking half the task. I would not really be trying to understand humans, but rather in a way, be standing in judgement of them. This is certainly not wise. And, suddenly, it stood in front me like a colossus demanding, "You need to live in wisdom! You need to live in wisdom!" This compelled me to try to do an examination of human nature, beginning with myself.

As I wrote, I ruminated over my writings, crystalising them into these brief quotes contained herein. Later, two friends convinced me to put some of these quotes in a collection as a book. And so, you are now holding " Living in wisdom – an examination of human nature" in your hands.

Formation and Organisation of This Book

This book has eleven sections covering as many subject areas. Looking at the content page, one may get the impression that these are disparate themes with no common thread connecting them. But once one begins to read, it will immediately become apparent that its central concern is the contemplation of human nature and our relation to it, whether through the observation of individuals as single entities, or through their actions as a part of specific groups, institutions, processes and systems; and then responding with wisdom. It therefore covers from the priest and religious believers, to the politician and government as a collective body, school teacher and schools, policeman and security forces, and the list goes on.

These eleven sections are set out randomly. I did not prioritise in any manner, because I am of the view that all of these behaviours are more or less of equal importance, and are interconnected in their expression of the nature of humans. I grouped these thoughts under these eleven headings with the sole purpose of having some sort of structure that would make it easier for readers to follow. The criterion used is that thoughts under each section, are generally closely related to the subject/title of that section.

In collecting these thoughts I did not set out to observe people in any specific field, or indeed any field at all. I simply observed them. Nothing in this work was written with any specific individual, group of individuals, or institution in mind, for as one quote says, it is easy for anyone to make a saint of himself and devils of everyone else. I therefore simply formulated into quotes what I sensed as I went about the business of interacting with people, in an effort to learn more about myself, my world, and what might be the best ways to relate to my fellowmen.

All the thoughts expressed herein are mine. However, no one develops anything from nothing. Therefore, apart from my observations as stated above, there are other sources of inspiration which must be recognised.

As noted above, while at university, I read many of the great philosophers, which must have influenced me in one way or the other. Further, as Dr. R. Mawuli Coffie, one of the reviewers of this book quite rightly decerned, this work is certainly heavily influenced by, and in some instances borrows from, the folk philosophy of the people and culture from which I hail. For example, I was taught from early childhood that "Sense make before book." In all my studies of philosophy, I have always been guided by that simple yet very profound saying of my Caribbean elders, most of whom it must be noted, knew little of literacy. It has empowered me to challenge every philosopher I have read, and every teacher of philosophy I have met. As I do, so too every Caribbean fisherman and farmer I am acquainted with, will earnestly challenge any Plato or Einstein without a second thought for their intellectual standing.

And then, the African DNA code that is the foundation of my being; consciously or unconsciously underpins my thinking. Our history of being victims of slavery, racism, colonialism, imperialism and poverty, is an ever-loud echo in my head, heart and soul, thanks in great part to the Black Power movement, and the energic young socialists who sprang up all over the Caribbean in the 70s and early 80s. The philosophical contents of the calypsos of Leroy "Black Stalin" Calliste, and Glenroy "Sulle" Caesar, and the profound revolutionary ideas expressed in the Roots Reggae of Bob Marley and The Wailers, are parts of the expressions of my people's wisdom that have literally sharpened and electrified my reasonings.

Still, this book was essentially formed from my observations of the series of different human relations, which determine a large part of objective reality, in the space I occupy with others as existences, actively involved in the process of living. Of course, this work is far from being objective by the mere fact that it is a record of my subjective understandings of these realities. It is my awareness of this subjectivism why the book is structured containing a space under each quote, titled, "My reasoning is:" There, readers are invited to write their views on my thoughts. They are not only encouraged to interrogate my thoughts, but more importantly, to do their individual examination of human nature, while reflecting on their own behaviours and how they are contributing to the shaping of their world. In short, readers are asked to join the author in reasoning about living the examined life. Therefore, in reading this book, it must always be remembered that every quote is about human living. The figurative language and metaphoric examples used herein are therefore purely a matter of literary style and practical examples.

The Sections of the Book

As intimated above, the sections of the book came about purely from the need of having to structure and organise the work so that readers are able to follow the same more easily. It was not a case where the author decided the themes, and then went about seeking observations to fit into them. Indeed, it was the complete other way around. Because of that approach, this sectionalisation cannot be said to be perfect. However, every effort was made to offer the best logical organisation of these thoughts.

A prima facie look reveals that each section addresses a theme or topic that affects daily lives in the here and now. Issues such as politics, justice, faith, and love are matters with which ordinary people are confronted daily. Knowing the truth. What is true? How to find truth? Who is speaking the truth?, have all become rather very serious questions on a global scale, due inter alia, to the outpouring of fake and false news on the many platforms of Social Media.

There are sections on hate and reason, two issues that are much more troubling than we seemed to be aware of. Indeed, the practice of politics in many countries today, gives full credit to the claim of American Henry Adams that the essence of politics is "the systematic organization of hatreds." Hateful eruptions have replaced reason in political quarrels (for discourse has been abandoned in many instances), among some states as well, leaving international morality without a leg to stand on; and leaving reason a bystander, never to be consulted or considered.

From ancient Greeks to present day, great thinkers on social issues have underlined the central role of politics in the ordinary person's life. However, there has always been the question of whether the mass of the people understand the nature and essence of politics. Is it fuelled purely by political tribal hatred in which they unwittingly participate?

Ideas on justice occupy a central place in the thoughts expressed in this book. One of the fundamental doubts slightly disguised herein, is whether the existing court systems are designed to deliver justice? The link of justice to peace and the role of truth in the dispensation of justice are however not camouflaged, but clearly stated. Of equal importance in this section of the work is the role of wisdom in ensuring justice. And while the book contains no definitions of many concepts used including wisdom, there is a very clear and simple understanding as to how one arrives at justice.

There are some profound thoughts on friendship, which may demand of readers an examination not only of their relations to others, but whether friendship is possible, not to mention if it actually exists. The book boldly proclaims that there is nothing more prone to deceit than friendship, and that loyalty and faithfulness are purchased commodities. While these are very troubling blanket statements, (and here again there are no clear definitions of the terminologies used), the readers must never forget that these positions were arrived at by the author, through observations of the behaviours of human beings in the world in which he lives, and that the understandings he uses here, are borrowed from folk philosophy, with which the common man is totally au fair.

It is of no little significance that there is a space after each quote for readers to pencil-in their thoughts. The said space is provided thanks to the firm conviction of the author that every thought, view, idea, written in this book not only could be questioned, but ought to be challenged once the reader sees the need so to do. Additionally, this is the space where readers are invited not merely to think, but to express their thoughts in a clear manner, for writing out the ideas that are in one's head, helps in crystalizing the same. I suppose you now fully understand why its first page declares this book to be Your Book.

The final section titled, "On living each day," once again underlines the fundamental reasons why this book was written and published. It is clear that the work requires readers to firstly begin to think, begin to question; enquire about the nature and essence of things like love, hate, friendship, politics and justice within the context of their lives in every material particular. In short, enquire about human nature as expressed through the various types of relations they experience. How do these expressions affect you? Can you live without them? If not, then how do you handle them once they are part of your daily life in one way or the other. And again, the inclusion of this element shows that this book is not about abstractions in thought, it is about practical living in the here and now.

Secondly, the book demands readers do serious introspection, and consider whether they are living or just existing? Some quotes proffer that life is merely existence, living is what fashions the biological being into a social human being, into a living existence, as distinct from an existence which happens to have life. This not just intimates, but rather emphasizes that living for the human should be understood as a never-ending process of communication and exchange with other humans, which leads to consequences. From this the question must be asked: What are the results of these exchanges and consequences on you the reader, and on the world you inhabit?

We must be concerned with these results, if only to know or try to understand the trajectory of change. One may argue that they make us better humans from a sociological standpoint. But this leads to further questions: In what way? For example, are we morally better? Have we made the world a better place? If so, how? Needless to say, gaging these results is no simple or straightforward matter.

This book was not written for philosophers, or teachers and dedicated students of philosophy. It therefore has no philosophical definitions, no references to great philosophical theories and the like. Further, as regards concepts and their definitions, this book takes the position that there are accepted common layman understandings of terms like peace and justice. For example, it is the view of the author that by the term good, it is commonly understood that the good-doer's actions or non-actions do not cause any harm to others, but in addition, are also beneficial to them. Based on these layman's understandings, the author arrived at the conclusion that there was no need for highfalutin philosophical definitions unnecessarily complicating a work, which is meant to inform, not confuse. The issue here is ordinary people's outlook on life, not arguing whether rationalists or empiricists have the correct epistemological theory.

The modest aim of this book is providing its readers with an understanding that life must be cherished as the foundation for living. Life is not living in and off itself. We must go further and find out: Why do we have life and for what? How are we living our lives? And, how do we live best with one another? These are key questions this book raises. In answering them using the, "My reasoning is:" section, it is hoped that readers will come to the idea of the need to live the examined life. And, so ask: is there need for change to make society better? Is there need for change in each of us as individuals to make us and therefore society better? If so, what should these changes be, and how do we effect them? If not, then why not?

And there are the more difficult questions: for example; what is meant by better? How do we judge that better?

The author does not pretend to have the answers to any of these questions. What the work does is pose them not in an abstract, atmospheric or tangential manner, but in a most direct way, in an effort to encourage the readers to seek answers by way of reason, and so refuse to let life simply happen to them, seeing that Socrates was right; "The un-examined life is not worth living."

Through this work, it is hoped that readers will be encouraged to go beyond the living of work and play, beyond the living of belief and emotions, to live the life of the mind daily. And, by so doing get a better understanding of human nature, but most importantly, a fuller understanding of their living.

Richard A. Byron-Cox

On Character

Birth happened to you, and death will happen to you. Life is your existence between these two points. Will you sail or will you drift? Will life also merely happen to you?

My reasoning is:

....
....
....
....
....
....
....
....

Strength is not always muscles and force. It is often the will and determination to succeed.

My reasoning is:

....
....
....
....
....
....
....
....

We make adjustments when we have people in our lives, be they man, woman, or child. But that must not stop us from living our essence.

My reasoning is:
....
....
....
....
....
....
....
....

Appreciating one's own imperfections and limitations is a measure of one's humility.

My reasoning is:
....
....
....
....
....
....
....
....

There is a special grace in humility that comes from great heights.

My reasoning is:

....
....
....
....
....
....
....
....

Individual/personal sovereignty of heart, mind, and soul must never be compromised.

My reasoning is:

....
....
....
....
....
....
....
....

Living in wisdom

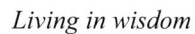

The noble will always seek truth, right, and justice for all.

My reasoning is:

....
....
....
....
....
....
....
....

Never sell your human dignity, for it is priceless!

My reasoning is:

....
....
....
....
....
....
....
....

Hold no discourse with insults to reason and intellect, disgraces to morality and nobility, and murderers of truth and honesty!

My reasoning is:

....
....
....
....
....
....
....
....

The only people who are afraid of the truth are those who want to continue living the lie.

My reasoning is:

....
....
....
....
....
....
....
....

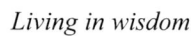

Your intellect blinds no one to your lack of human decency!

My reasoning is:

....
....
....
....
....
....
....
....

You cannot be standing up for your rights by practising wrongs against others.

My reasoning is:

....
....
....
....
....
....
....
....

The wise, good and gracious remember and are thankful for the one kindness rendered to them, while forgiving a million wrongs. The ingrates do the reverse.

My reasoning is:

....
....
....
....
....
....
....
....

The man who rejects the path of undeserved advantage, preferring that of honest service, can never be corrupted!

My reasoning is:

....
....
....
....
....
....
....
....

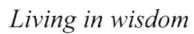

If loyalty means that I have to be deceitful, untruthful, and unjust, then yes, I am disloyal.

My reasoning is:
....
....
....
....
....
....
....
....

Integrity is like the laws of Physics; it is permanently true!

My reasoning is:
....
....
....
....
....
....
....
....

Most may be concerned with just your flaws. You must be concerned with your essence!

My reasoning is:
....
....
....
....
....
....
....
....

They who honour in service of the good, and who are honoured by having served the good, are of the greatest value to humanity.

My reasoning is:
....
....
....
....
....
....
....
....

Living in wisdom

John Donne admonishes that no man is an island.... Yet, there are moments when living forces us to be unbreakable rocks in splendid isolation.

My reasoning is:
....
....
....
....
....
....
....
....

It is facing challenging changes, situations, and circumstances that makes one fit for survival.

My reasoning is:
....
....
....
....
....
....
....
....

Living also means meeting adversities with determination.

My reasoning is:
....
....
....
....
....
....
....
....

Living is a constant conscious or unconscious battle, even for the privileged.

My reasoning is:
....
....
....
....
....
....
....
....

Substance must always be preferred over spectacle, unless there is only spectacle.

My reasoning is:

....
....
....
....
....
....
....
....

Your reasons to be on the down are sometimes real. And that is why you need to be on the up, because that's the only way you will change the situation!

My reasoning is:

....
....
....
....
....
....
....
....

The noble knows no honour can be had from lying.

My reasoning is:
....
....
....
....
....
....
....
....

Be extremely cautious in making judgements about people's character.

My reasoning is:
....
....
....
....
....
....
....
....

As a professional in your field of work, you never have difficult tasks; but, you are going to meet difficult people. Learn to deal with them!

My reasoning is:
....
....
....
....
....
....
....
....

On Courage

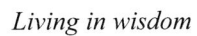

If you value your voice, let it be heard and understood.

My reasoning is:
....
....
....
....
....
....
....
....

For the righteously successful to have gotten where they are, they had to cross many turbulent rivers not spanned by bridges. They have paid their dues!

My reasoning is:
....
....
....
....
....
....
....
....

Aim for the stars, you might miss and hit the moon. Remember, a full moon is brilliant!

My reasoning is:
....
....
....
....
....
....
....
....

To live your life without courage, is to be a living dead!!

My reasoning is:
....
....
....
....
....
....
....
....

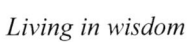

You can either lift you up, or drag you down. The choice is yours!

My reasoning is:
....
....
....
....
....
....
....
....

Courage can and may get you killed. But, you can be a coward, and so never live.

My reasoning is:
....
....
....
....
....
....
....
....

Life is full of challenges, and it should be so, because these are parts of what make us strong, wise, humble, and beautiful.

My reasoning is:
....
....
....
....
....
....
....
....

Some of the rivers people have crossed were made by their own tears.

My reasoning is:
....
....
....
....
....
....
....
....

Fight injustice wherever you meet it!

My reasoning is:
....
....
....
....
....
....
....
....

Integrity demands that we say and do what is right, knowing that some will make enemies of us because of it!

My reasoning is:
....
....
....
....
....
....
....
....

Glorious victories only come having undertaken arduous battles! It's a simple truism!

My reasoning is:

....
....
....
....
....
....
....
....

There is no courage until one is prepared to pay the price it costs!

My reasoning is:

....
....
....
....
....
....
....
....

Never surrender purely because of disappointments. Always remember these are in the nature of things, and of course people.

My reasoning is:
....
....
....
....
....
....
....
....

Exemplary courage is the rational relentless pursuit of justice in the face of brutal universal opposition!

My reasoning is:
....
....
....
....
....
....
....
....

Remember, quite often, you are all you have really, but self-pity is not the answer.

My reasoning is:
....
....
....
....
....
....
....
....

If you are determined never to be laughed at, then you lack the courage to be you.

My reasoning is:
....
....
....
....
....
....
....
....

Challenge is the path through which all champions have successfully trod.

My reasoning is:
....
....
....
....
....
....
....
....

The beauty of your success shall be the inspiration for someone's aspiration!

My reasoning is:
....
....
....
....
....
....
....
....

Fear is the chief author of lies!

My reasoning is:
....
....
....
....
....
....
....
....

Courage is born of reasoned conviction.

My reasoning is:
....
....
....
....
....
....
....
....

On Love

Love is intense in all its aspects, so when it hurts, it hurts intensely. It never hurts gently.

My reasoning is:

....
....
....
....
....
....
....
....

There can't be humanity without love!

My reasoning is:

....
....
....
....
....
....
....
....

For it is love, yes love that makes us better: the love we give and the love we receive.

My reasoning is:
....
....
....
....
....
....
....
....

Remember to open your heart so that love pours out, unlock your mind for wisdom to flow in, and carry a spirit of peace to the world! Yes, it all begins with love!

My reasoning is:
....
....
....
....
....
....
....
....

Sometimes your head has got to save you from your heart and soul. And sometimes, your heart and soul have got to put your head right!

My reasoning is:
....
....
....
....
....
....
....
....

A human void of sympathy, empathy, and love, is worse than a blood-thirsty, crazy beast!

My reasoning is:
....
....
....
....
....
....
....
....

Love is always disposed to reason.

My reasoning is:

....
....
....
....
....
....
....
....

No one with selflove will deny themselves peace, health and joy, holding on to the sick belief that hate is the source and meaning of life.

My reasoning is:

....
....
....
....
....
....
....
....

The absence of selflove makes many feel that happiness is in an abundance of paper money, and a mountain of material things.

My reasoning is:
....
....
....
....
....
....
....
....

The saddest, antisocial, most inhumane people one meets have one thing in common; no selflove. Nothing makes the human more depraved than the absence of selflove.

My reasoning is:
....
....
....
....
....
....
....
....

Often, souls pregnant with pains, give birth to spirits glowing with love and beauty.

My reasoning is:
....
....
....
....
....
....
....
....

Heartbreak is a desolate island, where even hope and faith may leave you abandoned. Sadly, love soon or later brings heartbreak!

My reasoning is:
....
....
....
....
....
....
....
....

Selflove ought not to be confused with the selfishness of egoism that characterizes the automized individual, a heartless and soulless existence.

My reasoning is:
....
....
....
....
....
....
....
....

There is no ugly flower. But some are poisonous, and therefore fatal to you!

My reasoning is:
....
....
....
....
....
....
....
....

Living in wisdom

Some people were so betrayed by love that they seek refuge in bitterness and hate.

My reasoning is:

....
....
....
....
....
....
....
....

Is it that love often escapes to another galaxy? Everybody is in the hunt, but very few if any, seem able to find it. Or is it that the great Trinidadian calypsonian, The Mighty Sparrow is right? "No money, no love!"

My reasoning is:

....
....
....
....
....
....
....
....

I have decided to stick with love because hate is too heavy, too painful, too ugly and too sadistic to carry on my shoulder on this journey of living.

My reasoning is:

....
....
....
....
....
....
....
....

On Reason

In wise judgements, emotions are vanquished by reason.

My reasoning is:

....
....
....
....
....
....
....
....

In getting it right, care is to be cherished over speed.

My reasoning is:

....
....
....
....
....
....
....
....

It is not stupid to be rational and reasonable in an irrational world, but it sure can be dangerous!

My reasoning is:
....
....
....
....
....
....
....
....

The intelligent must not just be above, but beyond fools, idiots and ignoramuses!

My reasoning is:
....
....
....
....
....
....
....
....

It's natural for the intelligent to combat ignorance, ignore irrelevance, and be contemptuous of stupidity!

My reasoning is:

....
....
....
....
....
....
....
....

What good is intelligence if one refuses to live intelligently?

My reasoning is:

....
....
....
....
....
....
....
....

Ignorance may be a doorway to knowledge, but stupidity is a never-ending journey to nowhere.

My reasoning is:
....
....
....
....
....
....
....
....

Never be too arrogant to learn.

My reasoning is:
....
....
....
....
....
....
....
....

Naivety could be cherished, even celebrated, but only in children! It is dangerous folly when found in people who should know better!

My reasoning is:

....
....
....
....
....
....
....
....

Ignorance adorns no one.

My reasoning is:

....
....
....
....
....
....
....
....

Stubbornness is not a sign of intelligence.

My reasoning is:
....
....
....
....
....
....
....
....

Refusing to interrogate the message, in preference to crucifying the messenger, is ignoring substance to embrace slander.

My reasoning is:
....
....
....
....
....
....
....
....

The chatter of a fool is not an opinion in the eyes of the wise.

My reasoning is:
....
....
....
....
....
....
....
....

Reason must bow to power, save when reason is that power.

My reasoning is:
....
....
....
....
....
....
....
....

A poverty of mind is the most common feature among humans today.

My reasoning is:

....
....
....
....
....
....
....
....

A man of reason prefers being chastised by one wise man, than to be praised by a billion fools.

My reasoning is:

....
....
....
....
....
....
....
....

Science never seeks to approve or disprove, to uplift or denigrate, to salute or mock. Its only mission is the pursuit and embrace of truth. Any deviation from this rule means, what is then termed science, is but disguised dogma!

My reasoning is:
....
....
....
....
....
....
....
....

Reason is rarely if ever found in the uncultured.

My reasoning is:
....
....
....
....
....
....
....
....

Living in wisdom

No need to dignify verbal rubbish regardless of the sort, or from whom it comes.

My reasoning is:
....
....
....
....
....
....
....
....

It's foolish to develop a difficult equation to arrive at a simple, existing solution.

My reasoning is:
....
....
....
....
....
....
....
....

Stupidity, regardless of how many mouths it, and how loud, is still stupidity!

My reasoning is:

....
....
....
....
....
....
....
....

Reason in the young is often lacking. Be patient with them.

My reasoning is:

....
....
....
....
....
....
....
....

Absurdity and stupidity are more commonplace than you could ever imagine!

My reasoning is:
....
....
....
....
....
....
....
....

It's right to be generally understanding and forgiving of the ignorant.

My reasoning is:
....
....
....
....
....
....
....
....

The brainless will see reason the day the Pope confesses his atheism.

My reasoning is:
....
....
....
....
....
....
....
....

Never be part of anything that dictates that you are not to use your brains!

My reasoning is:
....
....
....
....
....
....
....
....

Idiots will always try to draw you in. Be wise! Always leave them out!

My reasoning is:

....
....
....
....
....
....
....
....

The wise knows that once reason has taken flight, discourse is impossible.

My reasoning is:

....
....
....
....
....
....
....
....

The wise prefers discourse over dispute or argument. The fool knows not the difference!

My reasoning is:
....
....
....
....
....
....
....
....

No intelligent, conscious, conscientious, and noble man can be comfortable with, or accepting of the global status quo! It is incumbent upon him to revolt!

My reasoning is:
....
....
....
....
....
....
....
....

Living in wisdom

It may be that the dumb and ignorant do have their stories. It is however, not incumbent upon the wise to listen to the tales of fools.

My reasoning is:

....
....
....
....
....
....
....
....

People with super-great minds create and implement great ideas, helping to fashion the future.

My reasoning is:

....
....
....
....
....
....
....
....

Folly is the fool's paradise

My reasoning is:
....
....
....
....
....
....
....
....

While the wise can easily recognise stupidity, they are never able to understand it!

My reasoning is:
....
....
....
....
....
....
....
....

It is simply unfathomable that the racists accept variety in everything from trees and animals, to the styles of houses and cars. But, have a murderous hate for people with a different colour of skin and eyes, and different hair texture from their own. It there an explanation for this?!

My reasoning is:

....
....
....
....
....
....
....
....

The pen should be preferred over the sword, for ink is much cheaper than blood. But truth be told, blood is the ink in which most of history is written, thanks to the sword.

My reasoning is:

....
....
....
....
....
....
....
....

In any effort to have a holistic understanding of expressed thoughts, one must not just read the lines and between the lines. It is absolutely necessary to also read:

Above the lines
Below the lines
And most crucially,
Beyond the lines!

My reasoning is:

....
....
....
....
....
....
....
....
....
....
....
....
....
....
....
....

All too often we place emotions and desires ahead of reason and intelligence, resulting in us being bewildered, disillusioned, deceived, and hurt.

My reasoning is:

....
....
....
....
....
....
....
....

It's impossible to discuss your life and its meaning with mountains, oceans, rivers, trees, animals, or the seasons. For such examination, you need people. Here lies the difference between existing and living.

My reasoning is:

....
....
....
....
....
....
....
....

Are we now at the stage where the masses are happier with smart phones and AI than their own brains?!

My reasoning is:

....
....
....
....
....
....
....
....

If anyone respects you enough to listen to you for three minutes, that is listen not to disprove you, not to agree with you, not to respond to you, but purely to understand you; never waste their time!

My reasoning is:

....
....
....
....
....
....
....
....

On Justice

When justice is denied, peace will vanish.

My reasoning is:
....
....
....
....
....
....
....
....

Justice is the result when fairness and rightness are applied.

My reasoning is:
....
....
....
....
....
....
....
....

Bureaucracy does not see people, nor suffering. It blindly follows procedure.

My reasoning is:
....
....
....
....
....
....
....
....

Conscious black people, who are the children of the victims of the transatlantic slave trade, stand with every struggle for justice.

My reasoning is:
....
....
....
....
....
....
....
....

The unjust, the wicked, and the violent, are only afraid of violence that makes them powerless.

My reasoning is:
....
....
....
....
....
....
....
....

Justice must come before mercy if mercy is not to be corrupted.

My reasoning is:
....
....
....
....
....
....
....
....

Evil is like gangrene. Showing it mercy will lead ultimately to the death of the merciful. A society that fails to understand this, and uses legal technicalities and political mechanics to grants space to evil, has a total misconception of justice; is in mortal danger, and on the road to decadence.

My reasoning is:

....
....
....
....
....
....
....
....

There is a serious need in the world for courts of justice as opposed to courts where law is king, for there have always been unjust laws, as there were unjust kings.

My reasoning is:

....
....
....
....
....
....
....
....

Privilege might see suffering, but cannot feel and understand it.

My reasoning is:
....
....
....
....
....
....
....
....

The extraction of wisdom from the aged who lives the examined life, by the young, desiring a cultured mind and a righteous soul, has never been more indispensable, if reason and justice are to survive in this age and beyond.

My reasoning is:
....
....
....
....
....
....
....
....

To insist on the dispensation of necessary justice, is neither unjust, nor demanding too much!

My reasoning is:
....
....
....
....
....
....
....
....

About Religious Faith

It is easy to make a saint of oneself and devils of those we dislike.

My reasoning is:
....
....
....
....
....
....
....
....

Religion and power politics are neither good, nor beautiful.

My reasoning is:
....
....
....
....
....
....
....
....

The good is beautiful, and the beautiful is good. It's only by knowing and practicing these we can save this world.

My reasoning is:

....
....
....
....
....
....
....
....

Blind belief is never disposed to reason or truth.

My reasoning is:

....
....
....
....
....
....
....
....

The evolutionists uses the tools of history, biology, physical anthropology and so much more, yet they truthfully say there is but a theory of evolution. The believers used no tools, read one self-contradicting book, have no evidence, but insist, it is a proven law that man was created. As Bob Marley said, "We must know and not believe."

My reasoning is:

....
....
....
....
....
....
....
....

Strange, but for a holy book, the bible justifies more evils than any other single book. From genocide, rape, and unjust wars, to infidelity, punishment of the innocent, incest, the list goes on. Yet believers see nothing wrong with this book!

My reasoning is:

....
....
....
....
....
....
....
....

There is no divinity in your soul, when your actions are so manifestly unrighteous.

My reasoning is:

....
....
....
....
....
....
....
....

Until we give up Christianity, we will never know the nobility of being black, and will always accept the evil of white supremacy!

My reasoning is:

....
....
....
....
....
....
....
....

Seeking friendship with the gods will not secure immortality for man.

My reasoning is:

....
....
....
....
....
....
....
....

Seeing the truth and refusing to accept it, is not faith. Rather, it is lying to yourself, and being deceitful to others.

My reasoning is:

....
....
....
....
....
....
....
....

Believers are people claiming to see and know the multiverse, while being totally blindfolded!

My reasoning is:
....
....
....
....
....
....
....
....

It's an absolute fool who prefers beliefs and opinions over facts!

My reasoning is:
....
....
....
....
....
....
....
....

Surrendering to belief is easy. You do and say nothing. Then you are nothing!

My reasoning is:

....
....
....
....
....
....
....
....

Truth is a terror to many believers, because it unhouses and de-houses them from their palace of ignorance, and their shrine of mind-crippling superstitions!

My reasoning is:

....
....
....
....
....
....
....
....

The blindest to truth is the believer. He knows not, and refuses to know! Belief seals his ignorance.

My reasoning is:
....
....
....
....
....
....
....
....

Religion's primary mission is to hide the truth, and thereby confuse and control.

My reasoning is:
....
....
....
....
....
....
....
....

Have the courage to know and so reject fear, the basis of belief !

My reasoning is:

....
....
....
....
....
....
....
....

The day you learn the essence of your humanity, you will not need religion to make you moral.

My reasoning is:

....
....
....
....
....
....
....
....

Baseless fear is born of ignorance, and only breeds more of the same!

My reasoning is:
....
....
....
....
....
....
....
....

Let your practice be love, your creed peace, and your brotherhood all humanity, and you'll have no need for religion.

My reasoning is:
....
....
....
....
....
....
....
....

Living in wisdom

Remember, no man is tall enough to see over the fence of today into tomorrow. You must reason rather than believe.

My reasoning is:
....
....
....
....
....
....
....
....

History shows that humans have caused unquantifiable damage, and untold suffering in preferring religious beliefs over facts and science.

My reasoning is:
....
....
....
....
....
....
....
....

The postulation that religion has caused more damage to black people than slavery has great merit.

My reasoning is:
....
....
....
....
....
....
....
....

Money is the supreme and universal power. It is so powerful that God's fate and trust is placed in it as testified by the collection of tithes and offering in every church.

My reasoning is:
....
....
....
....
....
....
....
....

The Caribbean people for the most part, cannot imagine a society not based on belief in God.

My reasoning is:

....
....
....
....
....
....
....
....

No preacher/pastor or indeed member of the laity has ever followed the commandment given by Christ himself in Mathew 19:21. How does one reconcile that failure with having faith?

My reasoning is:

....
....
....
....
....
....
....
....

Not every scream from a mountain top is a righteous message

My reasoning is:
....
....
....
....
....
....
....
....

Think of it. Think carefully. Isn't your pretend faith a masquerade hiding your fear? Just a convenient lie?

My reasoning is:
....
....
....
....
....
....
....
....

On Truth

In the absence of truth, Justice will run out of gas.

My reasoning is:

....
....
....
....
....
....
....
....

If everyone has their own truth, is it possible to ever arrive at justice?

My reasoning is:

....
....
....
....
....
....
....
....

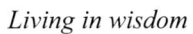

It seems we live in a world where one gender has a monopoly on truth.

My reasoning is:

....
....
....
....
....
....
....
....

The dues for joining the club of truth is pain.

My reasoning is:

....
....
....
....
....
....
....
....

The fear of truth is a most terrible burden to carry.

My reasoning is:

....
....
....
....
....
....
....
....

Truth is an unwelcomed alien in today's world! Speaking it is interpreted as a declaration of war by those who fear it.

My reasoning is:

....
....
....
....
....
....
....
....

The rumour mill is eternally the world's most active.

My reasoning is:

....
....
....
....
....
....
....
....

Truth is the acknowledgement of facts. Simple!

Therefore, to say truth is based on fact, is to say that something is added or taken away, thus making it something other than truth.

My reasoning is:

....
....
....
....
....
....
....
....

There is a choice: The truth that hurts but heals, or the lie that temporarily comforts, but ultimately ruins.

My reasoning is:

....
....
....
....
....
....
....
....

Truth is like an unpleasant but necessary medicine. Sometimes it tastes extremely bad, but it cures.

My reasoning is:

....
....
....
....
....
....
....
....

Truth is its own authority.

My reasoning is:

....
....
....
....
....
....
....
....

Most times, we only understand the essence of truth when we are forced to live it!

My reasoning is:

....
....
....
....
....
....
....
....

The fake, the vacuous, the mendacious, the envious, and the hateful despise the bearer of truth , seeing him as a frightening mirror to be smashed into a thousand fine pieces!

My reasoning is:

....
....
....
....
....
....
....
....

Unpleasant truth always enrages the liar and endangers the revealer!

My reasoning is:

....
....
....
....
....
....
....
....

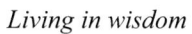

Truth is sometimes seen as evil because it often hurts, and no one loves pain.

My reasoning is:

....
....
....
....
....
....
....
....

May truth ever be our guide!

My reasoning is:

....
....
....
....
....
....
....
....

This first evidence of a man's independence and freedom is his courage to speak, hear, and live the truth, knowing that the consequence is being hated, ostracized, and living in the prison of loneliness.

My reasoning is:

....
....
....
....
....
....
....
....

If you are constantly concerned with the opinions of others, you will never be able to speak the truth!

My reasoning is:

....
....
....
....
....
....
....
....

On Politics

The altar of political correctness demands the sacrifice of truth, justice, peace, humanity, and ultimately love, as burnt offerings.

My reasoning is:

....
....
....
....
....
....
....
....

Honesty is not a principle in the practice of politics.

My reasoning is:

....
....
....
....
....
....
....
....

There is an all-consuming fury in the breast of the politician scorned, mocked, and rejected by the populace.

My reasoning is:

....
....
....
....
....
....
....
....

Morality is an irrelevance in this, the age of political correctness.

My reasoning is:

....
....
....
....
....
....
....
....

It's absolutely foolish to believe that in politics the court of public opinion is irrelevant.

My reasoning is:

....
....
....
....
....
....
....
....

Mudslinging is now sine qua non in politics universally.

My reasoning is:

....
....
....
....
....
....
....
....

A government that derails the pursuit of justice is morally decadent to its core.

My reasoning is:

....
....
....
....
....
....
....
....

Politicians claim the right to make promises, and the freedom to ignore those promises.

My reasoning is:

....
....
....
....
....
....
....
....

Political correctness needs no facts, only tolerance to come what may.

My reasoning is:

....
....
....
....
....
....
....
....

Generally, politics is only honest and decent in its dishonesty and indecency.

My reasoning is:

....
....
....
....
....
....
....
....

Claiming intention of preventing abuse by the majority in a democratic polity, there is now an endorsement of the tyranny against the majority and the state, not just by the minority, but by self-alienated and atomised individuals. This is insane!

My reasoning is:

....
....
....
....
....
....
....
....

On Friendship

If friendship finds you, you will have one of the rarest treasures, and experience one of the greatest wonders in all the multiverse.

My reasoning is:

....
....
....
....
....
....
....
....

Never give people a doorway to your life unless you know you mean something to them.

My reasoning is:

....
....
....
....
....
....
....
....

Friendship and humility occasioned by need, or conditioned by poverty, are dangerously false!

My reasoning is:

....
....
....
....
....
....
....
....

The key to your heart can do more damage than a dagger. You know the dagger, but you trust the key.

My reasoning is:

....
....
....
....
....
....
....
....

No decent and lasting relationship can be had without compromise.

My reasoning is:

....
....
....
....
....
....
....
....

A lesson you ought to learn from the storms of life is your role in sheltering your friends.

My reasoning is:

....
....
....
....
....
....
....
....

Cherish friendship, for it is what you have when all else is lost.

My reasoning is:

....
....
....
....
....
....
....
....

Good friends are like fine wines; with age the get better, and you enjoy them more.

My reasoning is:

....
....
....
....
....
....
....
....

Living in wisdom

Friendship is a corner stone in the living of a beautiful life.

My reasoning is:

....
....
....
....
....
....
....
....

Evil never laughs with, but always at you. Never smiled with it. It's not your friend!

My reasoning is:

....
....
....
....
....
....
....
....

Be careful when seeking friendship, for there is nothing more prone to deceit!

My reasoning is:

....
....
....
....
....
....
....
....

Befriending someone in their hour of need is one of the most gracious things one could ever do.

My reasoning is:

....
....
....
....
....
....
....
....

Stay as far as you can from inconsiderate people. Selfishness only sees self.

My reasoning is:

....
....
....
....
....
....
....
....

Know that 'friendly' mockery born of envy/jealousy is subtle enmity, and will fully manifest with time. Never be fooled by this mirage!

My reasoning is:

....
....
....
....
....
....
....
....

Unlike other challenges that may bend and even break you, betrayal shatters!! And while you may put some of the pieces back together, you are never totally whole again!! Betrayal is born of trust!

My reasoning is:

....
....
....
....
....
....
....
....

Before inviting people with baggage into your life, remember, overweight is very expensive!

My reasoning is:

....
....
....
....
....
....
....
....

Greed can never be satisfied. Don't become a host for natural parasites.

My reasoning is:

....
....
....
....
....
....
....
....

The self-centred consciously takes all of your time, but determinedly refuses to give any of theirs!

My reasoning is:

....
....
....
....
....
....
....
....

Naivety, self-sacrificing generosity, unconditional loyalty, and purchased fraternity, only lead to total bankruptcy. Remember, being good doesn't mean being foolish!

My reasoning is:

....
....
....
....
....
....
....
....

There's no Job among men! Loyalty and faithfulness are purchased commodities. People are loyal if there is profit to be gained, or interest to be protected. Otherwise, you are on your own.

My reasoning is:

....
....
....
....
....
....
....
....

One may be indifferent to loneliness, but knowing there is no one you can trust, brings inescapable absolute desolation.

My reasoning is:

....
....
....
....
....
....
....
....

If you have to choose between truth and your friends, then you are a sheep running with wolves!

My reasoning is:

....
....
....
....
....
....
....
....

The easiest things to buy are "friends." Just make sure you never run out of money!

My reasoning is:

..
....
....
....
....
....
....
....

Nothing is wrong in seeking friendship with those who worked tirelessly to be emblems of the standards we cherish.

My reasoning is:

....
....
....
....
....
....
....
....

Being a friend is ultimately a choice, because then, the words united we stand have real meaning.

My reasoning is:

....
....
....
....
....
....
....
....

On Hate

If you must hate; then target injustice, racism, sincere ignorance, and greed. But pity the practitioners of such iniquities.

My reasoning is:

....
....
....
....
....
....
....
....

Hate inevitably breeds a culture of violence.

My reasoning is:

....
....
....
....
....
....
....
....

Aggressive, deep-seated envy is all-consuming. Flee!

My reasoning is:

....
....
....
....
....
....
....
....

It's better to be silent than a drumbeater for hate.

My reasoning is:

....
....
....
....
....
....
....
....

Hate makes you relish and embrace the ugly, the nasty, and the despicable.

My reasoning is:

....
....
....
....
....
....
....
....

There is nothing that alienates like hate!

My reasoning is:

....
....
....
....
....
....
....
....

With no beauty in the soul, the head is a minefield of evil, the heart is impure, and the hands will forever be unclean. Nurture your soul with beauty!

My reasoning is:

....
....
....
....
....
....
....
....

One must never ever be a trumpet of hate!

My reasoning is:

....
....
....
....
....
....
....
....

Hate is a common response to unpleasant truth!

My reasoning is:

....
....
....
....
....
....
....
....

It is bad when others hurt us, but it is downright foolish to let hate for them dictate the course of one's life, such that personal peace and contentment never abide.

My reasoning is:

....
....
....
....
....
....
....
....

The community might be affected by your hate; not due to some power you hold, but from the stench of your decaying soul, for without love we are living dead.

My reasoning is:

....
....
....
....
....
....
....
....

Anything mixed with hate is a dangerous cocktail!

My reasoning is:

....
....
....
....
....
....
....
....

Your hate is born of pure envy.

My reasoning is:

....
....
....
....
....
....
....
....

There can be no personal peace if the soul is never at rest. Be sure, a hateful man is a turbulent soul, full of pain.

My reasoning is:

....
....
....
....
....
....
....
....

An interesting dynamic of hate is that when you think that you are finished with it, it has only now began with you!

My reasoning is:

....
....
....
....
....
....
....
....

Mistakes and accidents are born of ignorance, innocence, carelessness, or downright stupidity. Evil, is the child of willful, spiteful, wicked intentions realized! One is to be forgiven, the other to be dreaded!

My reasoning is:

....
....
....
....
....
....
....
....

Know that hate can never lift you up, can never show you light, can never bring you peace, and can never make you beautiful. It will only make you a living example of the completed picture of Dorian Gray!

My reasoning is:

....
....
....
....
....
....
....
....

The wise cannot cherish hate.

My reasoning is:

....
....
....
....
....
....
....
....

On Living Each Day

Without a passion for living, your life is merely an existence!

My reasoning is:

....
....
....
....
....
....
....
....

Live not trying to shake to the noise of the irrelevant, but dancing to the music of your own being!

My reasoning is:

....
....
....
....
....
....
....
....

The selfish, the hypocrite, the bogus and the wicked are real; so too is the good! The choice is yours!

My reasoning is:

....
....
....
....
....
....
....
....

Jackasses ought to be labelled, then ignored!

My reasoning is:

....
....
....
....
....
....
....
....

Laying blame is always the scapegoat for the delinquent, the negligent, the incompetent, and above all, the indolent!

My reasoning is:

....
....
....
....
....
....
....
....

The greater the spectacle, the lesser the substance!

My reasoning is:

....
....
....
....
....
....
....
....

In a world of constant speed, there is only time to bite and swallow. But chewing, tasting, and digesting are important. You need to slow down sometimes.

My reasoning is:

....
....
....
....
....
....
....
....

An independence of much foliage and little fruit is but an empty masquerade.

My reasoning is:

....
....
....
....
....
....
....
....

The right is not always good. The just is not always good. However, the good is always right and just.

My reasoning is:

....
....
....
....
....
....
....
....

There is no greater deceiver and flatterer of a man's talents, abilities, and integrity, than his oversized ego!

My reasoning is:

....
....
....
....
....
....
....
....

The advantage of age is something called experience!

My reasoning is:

....
....
....
....
....
....
....
....

Even when having all aces, it is wise to play your hand with great caution.

My reasoning is:

....
....
....
....
....
....
....
....

High and low standards both cost. The difference: One is an investment; the other, a sure loss!

My reasoning is:

....
....
....
....
....
....
....
....

Never give pessimism any time in your life, any space in your brain, or let it take any joy from your heart!

My reasoning is:

....
....
....
....
....
....
....
....

In doing good, you might not be able to change evil, but never let evil change you!

My reasoning is:

....
....
....
....
....
....
....
....

Success breeds contempt from the envious.

My reasoning is:

....
....
....
....
....
....
....
....

Living in wisdom

Tomorrow's people need us to stand up today!

My reasoning is:

....
....
....
....
....
....
....
....

The essence of artificial prettiness is pretence and deceit, hence the excessive decoration, misrepresentation, and false physical presentation.

My reasoning is:

....
....
....
....
....
....
....
....

Ingratitude, inhumanity, injustice, hate, profound stupidity, and greed, are things the humane should never be guilty of.

My reasoning is:

....
....
....
....
....
....
....
....

Great love for television, religion, and social media is deadly poison to a healthy mind!

My reasoning is:

....
....
....
....
....
....
....
....

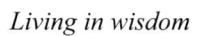

Genuine goodness always shines through, and could never be dimmed by the worst of evils!

My reasoning is:

....
....
....
....
....
....
....
....

The chains of religion offering to set you free are everywhere!

My reasoning is:

....
....
....
....
....
....
....
....

Buffoonery is a classic trait of intellectual nonentities.

My reasoning is:

....
....
....
....
....
....
....
....

Never let the ugly in others destroy the beauty in you.

My reasoning is:

....
....
....
....
....
....
....
....

The knowledge-driven assurance of the learned, is often labelled arrogance by the uninformed and envious. But as with all things, time and facts absolved the assured.

My reasoning is:

....
....
....
....
....
....
....
....

The beauty of your dream is in its realisation.

My reasoning is:

....
....
....
....
....
....
....
....

An ignorant utterance is not an opinion.

Belief is not knowledge.

Irrationality is not reason.

Stupidity is not wisdom.

There is therefore no arrogance in being dismissive of them all!

My reasoning is:

....
....
....
....
....
....
....
....

Rape, regardless of its nature is always a violation of the soul.

My reasoning is:

....
....
....
....
....
....
....
....

Never settle for the lesser evil, but always fight for the greater good.

My reasoning is:

....
....
....
....
....
....
....
....

In your haste to get things done, take time to ensure they aren't done wrong. Impatience is an enemy of excellence, not to mention perfection!

My reasoning is:

....
....
....
....
....
....
....
....

The idea that the so-called lesser evil is good is but a dangerous delusion. Evil is evil!

My reasoning is:

....
....
....
....
....
....
....
....

Passionate pursuit of your dream is an arduous and lonely mission.

My reasoning is:

....
....
....
....
....
....
....
....

You are not the first and will not be the last who went wrong. We are perfect only in our imperfection.

My reasoning is:

....
....
....
....
....
....
....
....

Reading must be part of your living. It makes your mind expand even when all physical growth has ceased.

My reasoning is:

....
....
....
....
....
....
....
....

Discipline is essential in the development of good character.

My reasoning is:

....
....
....
....
....
....
....
....

You only die if your teachings perish. Socrates and Dr. Martin Luther King Jr. et al will live once humanity does not perish! Their teachings belong to all times!

My reasoning is:

....
....
....
....
....
....
....
....

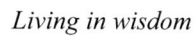

It's ludicrous to demand excellence from the mediocre.

My reasoning is:

....
....
....
....
....
....
....
....

A book is the hardest thing to sell to the average black man. Such a tragedy! You need to read!

My reasoning is:

....
....
....
....
....
....
....
....

If in utter desperation, you are visited by friendship and understanding, that visitor is love.

My reasoning is:

....
....
....
....
....
....
....
....

Living proves there's no shortcut to wisdom.

My reasoning is:

....
....
....
....
....
....
....
....

One must pardon oneself for yesteryears' misdeeds, and let go of anxieties of what the morrow would bring, to have complete peace.

My reasoning is:

....
....
....
....
....
....
....
....

Life is just existence. Living is what matters.

My reasoning is:

....
....
....
....
....
....
....
....

Living is the greatest learning institution to which we all have access. So live, but do so most attentively. For living is not merely the institution, it is the curriculum, the discipline, the teacher, the coach, the examiner, and the exam!

My reasoning is:

....
....
....
....
....
....
....
....

Wisdom must come before charity if charity is not to be abused.

My reasoning is:

....
....
....
....
....
....
....
....

Being patient is a profound exercise in discipline, self-control, maturity, and wisdom.

My reasoning is:

....
....
....
....
....
....
....
....

The sincerity of speech seeking gain is always doubtful, for its goal is profit; not declaring truth.

My reasoning is:

....
....
....
....
....
....
....
....

Yes, there are things money cannot buy, but it sure can purchase believable imitations, fabrications, and fictions of them. The real question therefore is whether people still cherish the things money cannot buy.

My reasoning is:

....
....
....
....
....
....
....
....

Criticizing is natural. Understanding is noble!

My reasoning is:

....
....
....
....
....
....
....
....

Death frightens only those who have failed to live!

My reasoning is:

....
....
....
....
....
....
....
....

Never sacrifice the future of children on the altar of being nice and wanting to be liked.

My reasoning is:

....
....
....
....
....
....
....
....

The souls of the good will never know peace, should they fail to stand up for truth and justice!

My reasoning is:

....
....
....
....
....
....
....
....

We always have time for the people and things we see as important to us.

My reasoning is:

....
....
....
....
....
....
....
....

Learning requires discipline. Ill-disciplined children will never learn.

My reasoning is:

....
....
....
....
....
....
....
....

These four decisions are absolutely crucial to living:
The career one chooses.
Whether one should get married.
The neighbourhood one chooses to live.
Whether to have children.
These can be seasonings or poisons to living.

My reasoning is:

....
....
....
....
....
....
....
....

Time does not make evil feeble. It makes it mature.

My reasoning is:

....
....
....
....
....
....
....
....

Never fall into the trap of thinking you are a hundred thousand times brighter than the sun. In fact, each of us is not even a twinkle in the darkest of night.

My reasoning is:

....
....
....
....
....
....
....
....

Bringing personal hate into daily life poisons everything.

My reasoning is:

....
....
....
....
....
....
....
....

Never let hurt rendered by the hand of ingratitude drain your heart of its love, your mind of its reason, and your soul of its beauty.

My reasoning is:

....
....
....
....
....
....
....
....

Never be afraid to change course if and when necessary. The story of the Titanic is lesson enough.

My reasoning is:

....
....
....
....
....
....
....
....

Your immediate world is your mirror. If you don't like the images you see reflected, cursing the mirror will not help!

My reasoning is:

....
....
....
....
....
....
....
....

Living in wisdom

Waking up is ultimately a matter of biological time, because one day you will not. Getting up is a decisive action born of desire and purpose.

Get up!

My reasoning is:

....
....
....
....
....
....
....
....

Don't believe them! You can change the world: in changing you, in helping someone, in just offering a smile. If there are a million trees and you plant one more, it will be a million and one! You have changed the world, just not the whole world. Light your candle now!

My reasoning is:

....
....
....
....
....
....
....
....

Specifically for the young:

In choosing a career, these must be the three central considerations:

You have love for it,

You have the talent to do it,

It can and will pay you!

My reasoning is:

....
....
....
....
....
....
....
....

The good that requires acknowledgement or recompense, is in essence a bribe.

My reasoning is:

....
....
....
....
....
....
....
....

Letting your emotions explode is like being an overheated machine. The greater that overheat, the graver the consequences.

My reasoning is:

....
....
....
....
....
....
....
....

Spring is but a dying memory. And yes, your summer may have passed, but that doesn't say you shouldn't make your autumn golden, and your winter warm. Life is most meaningful when lived fully.

My reasoning is:

....
....
....
....
....
....
....
....

Constantly and continuously aim for the ideal every day, but always live the real each minute! There is no moment in time more valuable than the present.

My reasoning is:

....
....
....
....
....
....
....
....

Find something to be excited about each day. It will move you from existing and surviving, to living, striving, and thriving every day.

My reasoning is:

....
....
....
....
....
....
....
....

There is no mystery as regards life's finale. Unlike a worm or a tree, every conscious sane human knows this. Therefore, what other proof is needed that living as opposed to existing is the human essence of life? The decisions each one must make is what life to live and how.

My reasoning is:

....
....
....
....
....
....
....
....

At the moment of your birth those around were smiling while you were crying. Live with the determination that when you die, those who knew you will be crying, while you will be smiling.

My reasoning is:

....
....
....
....
....
....
....
....

Afterword

It is much more than likely that after reading this work, you came away with more questions than answers. Be comforted that you have joined the company of most of the reviewers of this book. Be also comforted in knowing that it is a law of living that there will always be more questions than answers. Always.

If this book has helped to set you on the path of continuous/daily self-examination, it has achieved its main purpose, and you will at least know you better, and will from henceforth, be aware of your living way better than you did before. The saying that "We must be the change we want to see in this world," is attributed to Mahatma Ghandi. Whether he said it or not (there is no concrete evidence either way), it is something every person who lives the life of the mind most consider most seriously. We are truly serious about change when we begin with examining ourselves. Our personal conviction and determination must therefore be that "Practically, change begins with me examining my living, me living the life of the mind daily." This is the main thought I wanted all readers to get from this work.

In my journeys from my less-than-happy childhood to the challenges of adulthood; and from my tiny Caribbean island to the cosmopolises of Europe and North America, and to the great cities further afield including in Africa, and in Asia, I have always been treated as different; as something to be at least sceptical about. Sometimes bad, and other times, with little more than indifference, but never as part of any of those societies. My question was always: Why?

At first, I came to the unconsidered conclusion that this is all natural, after all, in China or India it was plain as daylight that I was physically different in appearance. But what of West Africa from where hailed the overriding majority of my ancestors, and where neither I, nor they, could perceive any physical difference whatsoever? Worse still, I am referred to as a "foreigner" in Barbados, my country of birth! Why is this so? One may say that the answer is rather easy, I speak differently. Well, I know many Barbadians who live there, and do not speak the Bajan lingo as good as I can; and, they are white, but they are not called foreigners.

Posing and considering the question why, as opposed to just jumping to a conclusion, forced me to examine this matter, taking into consideration the serious twist that while I am seen as a visitor or stranger in the other mentioned places, I am marked as a foreigner in the land of my birth!

These relations to me in both cases come from people speaking as individuals, and or as representatives of institutions, policies, practices, systems, traditions, laws, and much more. They express the interests and wishes of collectives of people which I am not part of. But, which I must interact with. They come from what is essential to me: living.

Any black person who travels regularly to non-black countries must have experienced at one time or the other being related to as an object. It is this latter factor of being an object, the other, the different, the unknown that demands that one must live the life of the mind, and find a way of changing the way these exchanges are conducted, so that they become relations of subject to subject. But how can this be effectively done? How does one move from being object to subject? This is why one must not just examine these situations, but examine self, as the crucial first step.

The above is about people in new situations and circumstances, and used here purely as an example. More commonly, even in one's own home, among family, while one may not be termed a stranger, (but there certainly are many cases when blood-relatives living together consider each other strangers), or a foreigner, ones is quite often the other. This also holds true in workplaces, social organisations, and other groupings and forms of collectives one may belong to. Because, the truth is, it is not difficult for one to be seen as the other as no two individuals are exactly alike.

The issue therefore is not trying to first and foremost deal with being the other, but addressing the phenomenon known in sociology and philosophy as alienation. Put in simple terms, one is or feels disconnected from the rest of the surrounding social environment, sometimes, all but totally. And, if there is any relation, it might not ever be mechanistic much more organic, -to use the terms of the French sociologist Emil Durkheim, but one of no meaningful connection with the society.

But as earlier said, this book is not about philosophical concepts and their understandings as important as these may be. It is about the individual's human relations, or more precisely, his understanding of them. And yet, it is more than that. It is in the end about being the best living you that you can be. The reason for this is as already given: Because living is why you have life.

Living is about your relations with people. Examining those relations is crucial if you want to make them the best they can be. And this means self-examining is central. Reading this work was supposed to have helped you to better understand this fact.

The work suggests through its quotes that in you mentally is where it all begins, but it doesn't stop there. This is one of the two key reasons why the "My reasoning is:" section was placed under each quote. The other being the readers' full freedom to challenge everything the author postulates. It is hoped that you fully employed both. If not, you need to, for you have not yet completed the process of making this book, Your Book.

The key point is about being wise enough to understand that you are at the centre of the examination of relations primarily concerning you. Because, your social relations is you living. Being conscious that you only exist socially, through relations, and not to constantly consider you and those relations, is to fail in living the life of the mind; is to fall asleep at the wheel when you are supposed to be not just driving, but doing so very attentively.

They who have life but fail to live are merely existing, actually denying life's essence, which is not just living, but living attentively, living the life of the body and the mind. Living the examined life. This is what you must do! Did you get that message?

Oh, as regards the question whether I have figured out the meaning and purpose of my life? You still haven't found that out after finishing the book?! Well, then you need to read the whole book again, for it simply means, you haven't figured out the real important question, which is: what is the meaning and purpose of your own life? Yes, your life is like a book, Your Book! Only you can write it! And in the same way this book is incomplete until you have examined your thoughts, and write your own verses, so too, your life really only turns into living when you examine it, and make it the best you can.

But, there is no need to worry, you have begun. Medical doctors have testified that quite often one must reexamine and reexamine, again and again in order to make the right diagnosis, and only then decide the right prescription. Still though, that is also not enough. One needs to go that crucial step and ensure proper application of the prescription!

This then is the call: Start living the examined life!

Richard A. Byron-Cox

Konigswinter

Germany

30/09/2025

Acknowledgement

As every writer knows, writing is generally a lonely undertaking. Not just physically, but in every sense of that term. In my personal case that loneliness is extreme as I basically do everything myself, from writing the first letter to seeing the work through to the publishers. Still, there are a few people who assisted me in one way or the other, and to whom I must express my sincere gratitude, here written in the chronological order of the creation of this work.

Firstly, this book might not have been written were it not for the advice of two friends. Ms Lydia Pope saw some of my sporadic postings of "Quotes by Richard A. Byron-Cox" on Social Media, and wrote to me encouraging that I put them together in a collection as a book. I responded that I would think about it. Sometime later, my friend since boyhood, Jeff "Jex" Roberts all but demanded that I write and publish this book, as in his view, there is just so much that I can share with the world if I were to do this. And so it came to pass that I put pen to paper -to use an old cliché, and this book became a reality. My sincerest thanks to them both for having motivated me to make that step.

My friend, Glenroy "Gobels" Phillips deserve my extra special thanks for suggesting that I make this book interactive. That great suggestion gave birth to the "My reasoning is:" space, which is found under each quote, allowing readers to express in writing, their own thoughts on the idea expressed in that specific quote.

All the reviewers have praised this feature of the book as something extra special, innovative, creative, and really valuable to readers.

I also offer extra special thanks to Dr. R. Mawuli Coffie, who played a key role in advising me as regards the design of this book. More than that he read the manuscript and wrote a very insightful review which is included in the early pages at the front of the book.

My sincere gratitude and deep appreciation are here extended to Vincentian historian of merit, Dr. Cleve McD Scott for writing an excellent forward, which captures the spirit, origin and most importantly, the mission of this work. I am honoured that an intellect of such capabilities graciously agreed to write the forward.

Very special thanks to Mr. Dexter Rose who read the manuscript and generously did some editing of the same. Dexter has always supported my literary efforts from the day I wrote the very first story for my first book.

Tremendous and deeply-heartfelt thanks to all the reviews of this work. Their wonderful reviews with their names attached, are found in the first few pages of the book. It is the least I could do to show genuine appreciation for them having given of their valuable time to read and assess this work, and then taking more time to pen their reviews. Each review is something very special to me, because each is a fundamental part of this work. I am indeed most appreciative!

Finally, I turn to family. I must say a very special thank you to my youngest sister Heather for being toally supportive, and for doing the close final edit of this work. Her insights have certainly improve this work. And, many thanks to my daughter Rose Angelica "Khandi" for always being my moral support, believing in me and my efforts, leaving no room for me to doubt myself should I ever have a thought of entertaining such. This moral support always lifts me up.

Richard A Byron-Cox
Konigswinter, Germany
30/09/2025

Made in the USA
Las Vegas, NV
24 November 2025